Journey with a

WARRIOR

WOMAN & MOM

Being Brave as Life's Journey Unfolds

Journey with a

WARRIOR
WOMAN & MOM

Tammy Durman

INSPIRED

Journey with a Warrior, Woman & Mom
First Edition, First Impression 2020
ISBN: 978-1-77630-662-6
Copyright © Tammy Durman
Published by:
Inspired Publishing
PO Box 82058 | Southdale | 2135
Johannesburg, South Africa
Email: info@inspiredpublishing.co.za

Contents

Dedication

My Abba father, all glory and honor to You, who will continue to see me through my journey.

My Mum and Dad, forever and always your love remains in my heart.

My Son Jordan Cole, you are my sunshine. Without you my life would not be complete. I love you. Always be strong and courageous and know that you can take anything on.

My Gorgeous sisters, Savi, Pam, Rosh & Jodi, and in loving memory of Kogs & Paddy. Thank you for your support and the role that you have played in my life. We share a love that will always be cherished.

My adorable brothers, Silva, Kris, Manu & Dean. Your love is forever and always.

My extended family: sister in laws, brother in laws, nephews, nieces and grand nephews and nieces. Life will always be meaningful with the insights you share.

My friends that have been an inspiration and shared some special moments with me, thank you.

CHAPTER ONE
FAITH, HOPE & LOVE

Faith, Hope & Love

"Faith, Hope and Love. They are priceless.
Lean in and find riches untold."
1 Corinthians 13:13

Tragedy gripped my heart at the age of Fifteen. I had lost my mom to cancer. The realization that mom was never going to be there for any of my "first's", like becoming a woman, my prize giving, my graduation, my wedding, the arrival of my baby. It was a devasting thought that continues to linger on. The shocking news that my elder sister Savi was shot during a robbery at their family home, ripped my and my family's hearts. My sister survived the ordeal but was left with the scars of that tragic incident. To this day the bullet is still lodged at the back of her neck.

In 2010, the daunting time loomed on. I sat in the courtroom holding back tears, as the judge declared the end of my marriage. The reality that I was a divorced woman began to kick in.

A maternal and feminine instinct began to rise within me and gave me the strength to continue my journey. That same strength allowed me to endure the sudden and unexpected death of my sister Kogs.

I tried to enter 2011 with as much hope as I could gather. Standing at the hospital emergency entrance, I watched hopelessly as my brother Dean was rushed in. We felt very little hope. Shortly after this incident, we were to face another tragedy. My brother Silva and his wife were knocked from behind in a car accident and he suffered a severe head injury.

Faith had to rise from within me, and I thank the Lord that both of my brothers survived through the faithful prayers and support from our family, pastors, leaders, friends & members of the church.

It felt as if all the hope that was left, was taken away. In 2019, we experienced the sudden death my dear sister Paddy. More recently in 2020 the unexpected stroke of my brother-in-law, and my Dad contracting the COVID19 virus at a high-risk age of 88 years left us shocked and afraid.

It begged the question, "Where was God in all this?" Yep! Don't we all ask ourselves this very same question? Well, He was there alright! The family rallied around each other to keep the faith, hope and love alive by unconditionally being there for each other.

Faith, hope and love was the Lord's promise to us that will remain engraved in our hearts. He has seen us through these tough and difficult times. In fact, 1 Corinthians 13 is our family motto and surprisingly our family's social media group name.

You, O Lord, keep my lamp burning, My God turns my darkness into Light.

- Psalm 18:28

There are many things in life that we cannot understand but we must trust God's judgement and be guided by His Hand.

Helen Steiner Rice

CHAPTER TWO
KEEP DREAMING

Keep Dreaming

Don't be afraid of the space between your dream and reality. If you can dream it, you can make it so. – Debra Davis

There is always a "suddenly" in your life's journey. This was mine. I had to take on responsibilities from the age 15 to help my dad and siblings to continue our lives without our mom.

The escape from my hard reality was school and church life, where I basically lost myself. Consumed with routine and activities, my life consisted entirely of house chores, cooking and cleaning.

I ventured into gymnastics, athletics, drum majorette, netball and the list goes on. I was nicknamed "Sporty", and the name has stuck with me to do this day. It came naturally to me when I ran the100 and 200-meter sprints, and relay was just the cherry on the top.

Having attained Victrix Ludorum in high school, and third place in the Eastern Transvaal Gymnastics, my dream was to represent my country in either one of these sports, but it was never realized because of the apartheid regime that South Africa was under at the time. It was another "suddenly" that made me realize I had to change my dream.

Do not give up, no matter what the challenge. Keep dreaming another God dream.

I was surrounded by friends in our neighborhood, school, and church. The church camps were great and contributed to a little bit of fun. It was a social life unlike any other. Most of the time it was our shared commitment and responsibilities to each other as a family.

As you move on in your journey, you realize what an awesome God we have and that if you ask for the right friends to surround you, He saves the best for last. I have recently had that encounter where I have the amazing friends that have crossed paths with me at the right time in my journey.

Reach high, for stars lie hidden in your soul.
Dream deep, for every dream precedes the goal.

– Pamela Vaull Starr

CHAPTER THREE
ARISE SHINE

Arise Shine

Arise Shine for your light has come, for all to see.
- Isaiah 60:1

Arise, Tammy!

These words echoed so loudly, the day I found out I was pregnant. During these 9 years, going through the motions and seeing specialist, we did test after test. I adjusted my diet and began marking off the calendar. It was all just too disheartening. We decided to leave it in the Lord's hands. Our family and Pastors continued praying faithfully for us.

Thinking back to the day I made the appointment for a checkup, I wanted to see the Doctor because it had been a week since I felt ill and I wasn't getting better.

I let the Doctor know how I was feeling inside, describing that it felt as if there was a bubble inside me which needed to be popped for me be okay. I didn't realize that my bubble was a teeny, tiny sized seed. Our 5-week-old baby's heart was pounding away in my womb.

It was confirmed as the Doctor smiled when he gave me a copy of the ultrasound. The joy I felt at that moment was overwhelming. The excitement continued, and the realization of motherhood for the next 40 weeks and thereafter was the happiest time of my life, with absolutely no complications. Hold fast for you too will have your miracle.

I can't wait to meet you for I already love you.

In the tiny petal of a tiny flower that grew from a tiny pod…Is the miracle and the mystery of all creation.

– Helen Steiner Rice

CHAPTER FOUR
BEND IN THE ROAD

Bend in the Road

Though the mountains be shaken and the hills be removed, yet MY unfailing love for you will not be shaken nor MY covenant of peace be removed, says the Lord, who has compassion on you. Isaiah 54:10

My divorce happened shortly after the birth our son. This was my bend in the road.

My fairytale wasn't going to end like they did in the books. *".. and they lived happily ever after"*. Instead, I literally had to take a bend in the road. With it came the difficult days, the happy moments, the early hours planning the day ahead. Like any single parent, you gear yourself up to take on the warrior stance, physically and mentally. Your unique strength is the sword you use to protect your family.

Like a warrior, I bravely took the road to continue my life's journey. Although it sometimes seemed that my prayers had not been heard. God always knew my every need.

The wonder woman instinct within me was unleashed during the day, and at night I was this beautifully mended porcelain that broke down in the stillness of the darkness, in the potter's hands.

Life changes around us. If you find that you've lost direction in the adventure of your lifetime, allow God to be your "GPS" and re-direct you to reach your destination. Let Him be your true north along the new path, like he was and will always be for me.

A bend in the road is not the end of the road....
unless you fail to make the turn

Cheerful thoughts, like sunbeams lighten up the darkest fears, for when the heart is happy there is no time for tears.

– Helen Steiner Rice

CHAPTER FIVE
BOY MOM

Boy Mom

Bring them up with the discipline and instruction that comes from the lord
Ephesians 6:4

As a boy mom, you know that each day with your son is exciting and different. You are treasured and showered with an overwhelming love. I enjoyed raising my son single handedly with grace and strength from God.

For me, it was my metanoia journey of change, mind, heart, and self that helped me. It is not easy being on this journey, but it certainly is worth it – even during the challenging teenage years.

Don't get me wrong, it wasn't all smooth sailing all the time. There were the shopping moments, never ending toys lying around to this day, an untidy room with clothes scattered everywhere, girl crushes, (yes! you read right) the nagging and shouting moments. But what makes it all the worthwhile is the unexpected random hugs and kisses. The, "you're the best mum in the whole world", and little cards, drawings, gifts made at school. The late nights making cupcakes and cute gift parcels for his classmates that we made for every single birthday. The achievements and days of being the cheerleader at soccer games and concerts is priceless.

That is how you know a *boy mum*, by all the tears and joy that she experiences all at once. Rock being a boy mum, they are our Princes until they become Kings one day.

You will always be the miracle that makes my life complete.

So many times, you feel like you failed,
but in the eyes, heart & mind of your child
you are supermom.
– S Precourt

CHAPTER SIX
TODAY IS THE DAY

Today is the Day

Commit to the Lord whatever you do, and your plans will succeed

Proverbs 16:3

At the dawn of sunrise, wake up to a wonder of expectation that says *"today is the day."* Begin your day with a grateful heart, spending that time in prayer and reading your bible or daily plan and devotion. Use that confession to pause during the day and say it to yourself out loud.

It creates an excitement to start your day with an overwhelmingly positive attitude. It equips you with confidence that you can take on the day, despite the challenges you may face.

I recall listening to a message at church; the Pastor read a poem he wrote titled "*Today is day*". It's the kind of sermon we all get to experience. The kind that leaves your heart pounding once you realize that it was meant for you. Yeah, this was meant for me.

It got me through the toughest times when I replayed the recording of the poem. It inspired me in all areas of my life including the corporate world. There were many "***today is the day***" moments for me.

When I reflected on my journey; past and present, I knew for sure that there was a bright future ahead of me.

Make today the day for you. I do not know where you are at this very moment but know that if you are reading this chapter it is no coincidence. Allow it to inspire you, step into who you are meant to be.

Courage isn't having the strength to go on
It is going on when you don't have strength.

If you must look back, do so forgivingly.

If you must look forward,

do so prayerfully.

However, the wisest thing you can do

is be present in the

present ......gratefully.

– Maya Angelou

CHAPTER SEVEN
AUTHENTICITY

Authenticity

You armed me with strength for battle; you humbled my adversaries before me. Psalms 18:39

Like the analogy; thrown in the deep end, you begin to find a way to swim. But you have to keep moving so you do not sink into your loneliness and self-pity state.

It is not easy being a single woman in a corporate world, a couple's world or a co-parenting world. Handling your finances, making all of the big decisions on your own takes guts, but if you aren't brave, you will find yourself beginning to stay low and keeping it safe.

So, take the risk! Be *authentic*, mellow on one side and the hurricane on the other. You will begin to find a way to navigate those emotions and mindset. Rise up, and choose to adjust your sails and let the wind push you forward.

My personal journey saw me achieving dream after dream, like getting my drivers license and buying and paying off my brand new car by myself in a much different way than I had imagined or anticipated. I did however start by setting goals for myself. Completing my studies, becoming a manager, were goals I had listed for my career path Nothing can take that feeling of accomplishment away from you.

Through God's grace I chose to learn, grow and set goals every year no matter how big or small. Even renovations (hahaha) should be set as a goal to achieve. Every goal you take on will cost you in ways unique to you. It helps when you are organized and plan wisely, ultimately achieving your destiny and purpose.

You will have your challenges along the way; take it as an opportunity. Whenever you find your critics taking the wind out of your sails, adjust and re-group. If you need to let your anchor down do that, so that you can find your authentic self again.

*Start over and **set sail.***

You can have a mental transformation

in the same way as a physical

transformation.

– Gilian Gork

CHAPTER EIGHT
LOCKDOWN

Lockdown

COVID19 hit the world and I wasn't going to miss the chance of canvassing this time of our lives. Every single one of us have a deep passion inside of us, waiting to be unleashed.

No matter how that passion is exploded, it sets your world on fire. I had my moments of explosion, and it ignited and rekindled that fire within me. I was inspired and never looked back. Like the song *"this girl is on fire."* You better believe this girl had her feet on the ground.

The new world of lockdown had everyone figuring out their passion. You were able to do many different tasks, ideas and be an innovative entrepreneur in the "new normal" that we all have had to embrace during this time. The little things like connecting with family and friends took on a different meaning, including working and homeschooling online. Would it be worth it? I think so?

We adapted and became resilient. I grasped every skill that I needed to survive. Never remain in "lockdown" in any situation, believe in yourself, be brave, adapt and be resilient.

Every next level of your life will demand a different you.

Remind yourself of what you've been
able to overcome.
All the times you feel like you weren't going
to make it through. You proved many and
yourself wrong, you are
more powerful than you think.

- A Alves

CHAPTER NINE
MUSIC IS MY ESCAPE

Music is my Escape

I will praise you, Lord, with all my heart; I will tell of all the marvelous things you have done. Psalms 9:1

In this ever changing reality it is important to hold onto something constant; Jesus should be our true North.

From the time music filled my soul, it will always be my escape, my praise & worship, my exercise fix.

My family and friends know that if there is a message or function, there must be a song dedication from me. Like they say, when words cannot speak music will.

My kitchen has become my dance floor. When you hear your favorite song playing on the radio, I always say "turn up the volume and dance". Unwind! Whether it is my exercise routine or a dance beat, reminiscing when that song is played will fill your heart and home with that joy.

Music has touched my heart in so many ways especially when days seem long, or tough.

Where do you go to escape and re-group, or what do you do in a positive way to unwind when you are overwhelmed? Keep doing it! That is what makes us happy living life to its fullest.

We can't always choose the music life plays for us.
But we can choose how we dance to it.

A bird doesn't sing because it has an answer,
It sings because it has a song.

- Maya Angelou

CHAPTER TEN
LET IT GO FOR BETTER

Let it go for Better

"For I know the plans I have for you," declares the LORD, "plans to prosper you and not to harm you, plans to give you hope and a future". Jer 29:11

How reassuring it is to know that God's promises for each one of us is true. I have adopted that stance, and continuously declared these profound words. In all of my experiences. I ask myself these questions: "What have I learnt?" and "what do I need to let go?", in each of the difficult challenges I encounter, when our faith is tested, and the way we react or respond will determine the level of strength we have. My mum always said that problems should make us better and not bitter.

May this book inspire you, to accomplish your dreams, take that first step and let God do the rest. Let it also be a reminder that behind that cloud there is a silver lining. The Lord surely made the impossible, possible in my life. I know He can do the same for you. At the end of each chapter of your life, no matter how it turned out, let it go for better.

The Best is Yet to Come. 1 Corinthians 2-9

A journey of a thousand miles begins

with a single step.

Lao Tzu